English made easy

Key Stage 2
ages 9-10
Workbook 1

Author
John Hesk

DK

LONDON • NEW YORK • SYDNEY • DELHI

Spelling patterns

Look at these words and the different ways their **plurals** are formed:

dog	dogs
kiss	kisses
dish	dishes
church	churches
knife	knives
fly	flies
boy	boys

Now write the **plurals** of the words below. Use the examples above as a guide.
Check your answers in a dictionary. D
Remember: **Plural** means that there is more than one of something.

cat ....

ash ....

batch ....

wife ....

trolley ....

party ....

cry ....

toy ....

tray ....

key ....

parrot ....

lash ....

stitch ....

thief ....

lolly ....

aunty ....

berry ....

cake ....

day ....

monkey ....

hamster ....

sash ....

arch ....

leaf ....

dolly ....

shanty ....

try ....

alloy ....

bay ....

chimney ....

More on plurals

Complete the following rules.

How to make plurals

1 For most **nouns**, simply add ....

2 If the **noun** ends with **-s**, **-sh** or **-ch**, add ....

3 For most **nouns** ending with an **-f**, change the **f** to ...., and then add ....

4 If the **noun** ends with **-ly**, **-ry** or **-ty**, change the .... to ...., and then add ....

5 If the **noun ends** with **-ay**, **-ey**, **-oy**, just add ....

Find examples of **nouns** that end in each of the ways described above.
Write the words as both **singular** and **plural** nouns.
Remember: A **noun** is a naming word.

1 ....

2 ....

3 ....

4 ....

5 ....

Peculiar plurals!

Add **-es** to these words.

potato .... echo .... tomato ....

Add only **-s** to these words:

solo .... photo .... piano ....

Zulu .... banana .... kiwi ....

An alphabet of plurals

Can you write the **plurals** of the words in this alphabetical list? D

alley	....	net	....
box	....	orange	....
calf	....	pastry	....
donkey	....	quarry	....
elf	....	ray	....
fairy	....	story	....
gnu	....	torpedo	....
half	....	umbrella	....
igloo	....	volcano	....
jelly	....	worry	....
knight	....	xylophone	....
laugh	....	yacht	....
miss	....	zoo	....

Rewrite these nonsense sentences, and make all the **nouns plural**. D
Remember: A **noun** is a naming word.

The gnu in a tutu flew past the Zulu.

....

....

The tomato sang a solo while playing the piano.

....

....

Prefixes

Read the **definitions** below, and complete the explanation of each **prefix**. Check your answers in a dictionary. The first one has been done for you. D

Remember: A **prefix** is a group of letters added to the beginning of a word to change its meaning.

automatic: able to work by itself
autograph: a person's name written by him or herself

auto- means self ....

bicycle: a two-wheeled cycle
biped: a creature with two feet

bi- means ....

telephone: an instrument for sending and receiving sounds over a distance
telescope: an instrument for making distant objects appear nearer

tele- means ....

transport: carry from one place to another
transform: change from one thing to another

trans- means ....

circumference: distance around a circle
circumnavigate: sail or fly around something

circum- means ....

A collection of synonyms

Use a **thesaurus** or a **dictionary** to help you find at least two words that are the same or similar in meaning to these words. D T

Remember: **Synonyms** are words that have the same or similar meanings.

happy ....

sad ....

angry ....

calm ....

strong ....

weak ....

rough ....

smooth ....

quick ....

slow ....

Using synonyms

For each **adjective** listed below, write a sentence that uses at least two of the **synonyms** you wrote on page 6. Try to show the slight difference in meaning between your **synonyms**.

happy I was **pleased** with my card
and **delighted** with my presents.

sad ....

....

angry ....

....

calm ....

....

strong ....

....

weak ....

....

rough ....

....

smooth ....

....

quick ....

....

slow ....

....

Sayings

Read these **sayings**, then explain what each one means.

out of the frying pan into the fire means

over the top means

raining cats and dogs means

a storm in a teacup means

to blow your own trumpet means

to hit the nail on the head means

Picture that!

Now imagine that these **sayings** mean exactly what the words say – that they are **literal** rather than **metaphorical.** Choose two of the **sayings**, and draw a picture to illustrate their **literal** meaning. Write each **saying** under its picture.

Word-building

The **root** of the words below is **perfect**.

perfection   im**perfect**   **perfect**ly

Underline the **roots** in these words.

admit	permit	transmit
dictionary	predict	dictate
fixture	prefix	suffix

Now add the **root** of the first word in each line to the other words in the line to build more words with the same **root**.

report	trans __ __ __ __	ex __ __ __ __	__ __ __ __ able
inform	in __ __ __ __ ation	trans __ __ __ __	trans __ __ __ __ ation
defect	in __ __ __ __	in __ __ __ __ ion	af __ __ __ __ ion

Use each word you built above in a **sentence** that shows you understand its meaning.

....

....

....

....

....

....

....

....

....

Adverbs

Written dialogue can tell readers **how** things are said. Kenneth Grahame used these six **adverbs** in the following conversation from *The Wind in the Willows*:
slowly, **triumphantly**, **wistfully**, **doggedly**, **loyally**, **imploringly**.

Decide where each word would make the best sense, and write it in place. D
Remember: **Adverbs** tell us more about the verbs in a sentence.

1 It was indeed very compact and comfortable. Little sleeping-bunks – a little table that folded up against the wall – a cooking-stove, lockers, bookshelves, a bird cage with a bird in it; and pots, pans, jugs and kettles of every size and variety.

2 "All complete!" said the Toad .... , pulling open a locker. "You see – biscuits, potted lobster, sardines – everything you can possibly want. Soda-water here – baccy there – letter-paper, bacon, jam, cards and dominoes – you'll find," he continued, as they descended the steps again, "you'll find that nothing whatever has been forgotten, when we make our start this afternoon."

3 "I beg your pardon," said the Rat .... , as he chewed a straw, "but did I overhear you say something about '*we*', and '*start*', and '*this afternoon*'?"

4 "Now, you dear good old Ratty," said Toad .... , "don't begin talking in that stiff and sniffy sort of way, because you know you've *got* to come. I can't possibly manage without you, so please consider it settled, and don't argue – it's the one thing I can't stand. You surely don't mean to stick to your dull fusty old river all your life, and just live in a hole in a bank, and *boat*? I want to show you the world! I'm going to make an *animal* of you, my boy!"

5 "I don't care," said the Rat .... "I'm not coming, and that's flat. And I *am* going to stick to my old river, *and* live in a hole, *and* boat, as I've always done. And what's more, Mole's going to stick to me and do as I do, aren't you, Mole?"

6 "Of course I am," said the Mole .... "I'll always stick to you, Rat, and what you say is to be – has got to be. All the same, it sounds as if it might have been – well, rather fun, you know!" he added .... Poor Mole! The Life Adventurous was so new a thing to him and so thrilling; and this fresh aspect of it was so tempting; and he had fallen in love at first sight with the canary-coloured cart and all its little fitments.

Tenses

Verbs tell us whether an event has already happened, is happening now or will happen later.

Past tense	**Present tense**	**Future tense**
Toad escaped ...	Toad escapes ...	Toad will escape ...
Toad was escaping ...	Toad is escaping ...	

Rewrite these sentences, and choose a **verb** in the **tense** suggested.

Toad (future) his car.

....

Rat (present) by the river.

....

Mole (past) the door.

....

He (past) the caravan canary-yellow.

....

Toad (future) from prison.

....

The stoats and weasels (future) all Toad's belongings.

....

Toad (past) the policeman.

....

Badger (present) in the Wild Wood.

....

Writing dialogue

Look back at page 10, then complete the following sentences.

When each character starts to s _ _ _ _ _, a new p _ _ _ _ _ _ _ _ _ begins.

The actual words s _ _ _ _ _ _ are enclosed in s _ _ _ _ _ _ m _ _ _ _ _, which are also called i _ _ _ _ _ _ _ _ _ c _ _ _ _ _ _ _ .

Verbs such as **said** and **remarked** are separated from the speaker's words by c _ _ _ _ _ _ unless there are other punctuation marks in the speech.

When **reporting** what was said (rather than writing down the speaker's actual words) don't use s _ _ _ _ _ _ _ m _ _ _ _ _ .

Now use **reported speech** to write out what Rat and Mole said in paragraphs 5 and 6 on page 10.
Remember: **Reported speech** is what you would use if you were telling someone else about the conversation.

The rat replied doggedly that he didn't care and he wasn't going. He

More reported speech

Use **reported speech** to rewrite paragraph 2 of *The Wind in the Willows* on page 10.

When you change the characters' actual words (**direct speech**) into **reported speech**, what happens to the **verbs**?

Did you have to change anything else?

Correcting mistakes

Rewrite the sentences below, correcting the grammatical mistakes.

Toad said there wasn't nothing like it. It is the best pastime ever.

At first Rat says he weren't going nowhere.

Rat and Mole was persuaded to take a trip in Toad's caravan.

Starting a story

There are many different ways to **begin** a story. Kenneth Grahame starts *The Wind in the Willows* like this:

> "The Mole had been working very hard all the morning, spring-cleaning his little home."

J. R. R. Tolkien's *The Hobbit* begins like this:

> "In a hole in the ground there lived a hobbit. Not a nasty, dirty, wet hole, filled with the ends of worms and an oozy smell, nor yet a dry, bare, sandy hole with nothing in it to sit down on or to eat: it was a hobbit-hole, and that means comfort."

Robert Louis Stevenson begins *Treasure Island* like this:

> "Squire Trelawney, Dr. Livesey, and the rest of these gentlemen having asked me to write down the whole particulars about Treasure Island, from the beginning to the end, ... "

Which of these novels begins in the **middle** of something happening?

....

Which story is told by a character **after** the story has happened?

....

Which of these books starts with a **description** of the place where the story begins?

....

Different beginnings

Supposing the writers of the stories discussed on page 14 had decided to **begin** their famous books differently, how might they have **begun**?

If you have read these books, write a different **beginning** for each one. Otherwise, choose stories that **begin** in similar ways, and use a different style to write a new **beginning** for each one.

The Wind in the Willows or ....

The Hobbit or ....

Treasure Island or ....

Characters

How do we get to know the **personality** of a **character** in a story?
Tick the possible ways on this checklist.

- use the table of contents ☐
- character's description ☐
- what the character says ☐
- use the index ☐
- what other characters say ☐
- look at chapter headings ☐
- what the character does ☐
- how he or she treats others ☐
- look at the pictures ☐

Choose a **character** from a story you have read. Using the ways you have ticked in the checklist, make brief **notes** about the **character** here.

The character is called ....

He/she is in the story titled ....

written by ....

Notes

....

....

....

....

....

....

....

....

....

....

....

Add an incident!

Reread the notes you made on page 16. Now **plan** and then write an extra **incident** in the life of the **character** you chose.

Hints:
First decide how this **incident** will show us more about the **character**.
Then decide on one or two other **characters** to take part in the **incident**.
Think of a good **moment** in the story for the incident to happen.
Think of a **title** for the **incident**.

.... (title)

Patterns in a poem

Read this **poem** aloud.

The Land of Counterpane

When I was sick and lay a-bed,
I had two pillows at my head,
And all my toys beside me lay
To keep me happy all the day.

And sometimes for an hour or so
I watched my leaden soldiers go,
With different uniforms and drills,
Among the bed-clothes, through the hills;

And sometimes sent my ships in fleets
All up and down among the sheets;
Or brought my trees and houses out,
And planted cities all about.

I was the giant great and still
That sits upon the pillow-hill,
And sees before him dale and plain,
The pleasant land of counterpane.

Robert Louis Stevenson

This **poem** has a regular **rhythm**. Count the number of **beats** (syllables) in each line.

The number of **beats** in each line of the poem is ....

The Land of Counterpane has a simple pattern of **rhymes**.

Describe the **rhyming** scheme (pattern) of this poem.

....

....

Make a list of this poem's **rhyming pairs**.

....

....

More patterns in a poem

Read this **poem** aloud.

Escape at Bedtime

The lights from the parlour and kitchen shone out
Through the blinds and the windows and bars;
And high overhead and all moving about,
There were thousands of millions of stars.
There ne'er were such thousands of leaves on a tree,
Nor of people in church or the Park,
As the crowds of the stars that looked down upon me,
And that glittered and winked in the dark.

The Dog, and the Plough, and the Hunter, and all,
And the star of the sailor, and Mars,
These shone in the sky, and the pail by the wall
Would be half full of water and stars.
They saw me at last, and they chased me with cries,
And they soon had me packed into bed;
But the glory kept shining and bright in my eyes,
And the stars going round in my head.

Robert Louis Stevenson

There are two **rhythmic patterns** in *Escape at Bedtime*. The two numbers of **beats** (syllables) in the poem are .... and ....

Escape at Bedtime has a slightly different **rhyming scheme** from *The Land of Counterpane* on page 18. Describe the **rhyming scheme** of *Escape at Bedtime*.

Make a list of this poem's **rhyming pairs**.

Can you find anything in the two **poems** to suggest they were written by the same poet?

Looking at poems

Reread the **poem** *The Land of Counterpane* on page 18, then answer these questions.

Counterpane is an old-fashioned word. What is a counterpane? D

....

Name the metal from which the toy soldiers were made. Explain why you think this metal is no longer used for making toys.

....

....

Why does the boy call himself "the giant"?

....

What do the words **dale** and **plain** mean? D

....

....

Now reread the **poem** *Escape at Bedtime* on page 19, and answer these questions.

What is a parlour? D

....

The number of stars is compared with three things in the speaker's own experience. What are they?

....

....

Explain what is meant by "The Dog, and the Plough, and the Hunter".

....

Which words tell you that when he went to bed, he remembered the way the sky looked?

....

....

Reading and understanding

Read this **biography** of Robert Louis Stevenson, then answer the following questions in full sentences.

Robert Louis Stevenson was born in Edinburgh, Scotland, in the middle of the nineteenth century. His father was an engineer, well known for designing and building lighthouses. Robert was to become even more famous than his father, not as an engineer, but as an author.

When he was young, Robert's family hoped that he would follow in his father's footsteps, but very poor health made this impossible. Even as a child, Robert was often ill and had to spend a great deal of time in bed.

As a young man, Robert Louis Stevenson studied law and qualified as a barrister, but having set his heart on becoming an author, he put all his efforts into writing.

As an adult, he continued to suffer from tuberculosis, a serious chest ailment, and spent much time travelling in Europe and America, seeking warmer climates, where he thought his health might improve.

In 1880, after marrying in California, he and his wife returned to England. They settled there for a while, until in 1888, they went off to the South Pacific. Finally, the Stevensons settled in Samoa, and at first, Robert felt much healthier.

In 1894, however, the man whose books were loved by many throughout the world and who was called Tusitala (the storyteller) by the Samoan Islanders, died suddenly.

Robert Louis Stevenson wrote stories, poems, travel books and several novels. Two of his most famous books are *Treasure Island* and *Kidnapped*. Many of the poems from *A Child's Garden of Verses* are well known and well loved, remaining popular today, over one hundred years after Robert Louis Stevenson first wrote them.

Why is Robert Louis Stevenson famous?

....

....

When and where was he born, and when and where did he die?

....

....

Why did Robert Louis Stevenson often have to stay in bed when he was a boy?

....

....

Reading and understanding

Read the **biography** of Robert Louis Stevenson on page 21 again, then answer the following questions.

Why did Robert Louis Stevenson travel to different countries?

....

Where did he go in 1888?

....

Why do you think he was called **Tusitala**?

....

Explain what these **expressions** mean:

follow in his father's footsteps

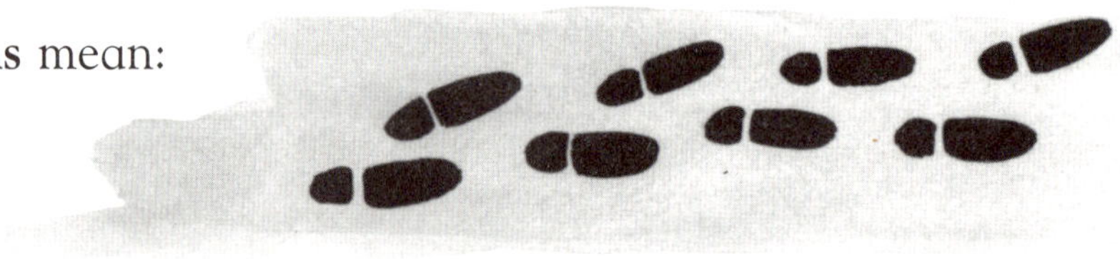

....

set his heart on

....

What do you notice about the way the events in Robert Louis Stevenson's life are arranged on the page?

....

....

This is a short **biography** of Robert Louis Stevenson. Give the meaning of the word **biography**. If necessary, use a dictionary. D

....

....

Now make up **three extra questions** that could be answered by using this **biography**.

....

....

....

Write a biography

Using the **biography** on page 21 as a guide, write your own **biography** about a famous person who interests you. You will need to make short **notes** from **reference** books, **CD-ROMs,** the **Internet** or your own knowledge. Take **notes** from more than one place if possible.

Remember: Use a new **paragraph** for each new point of information.

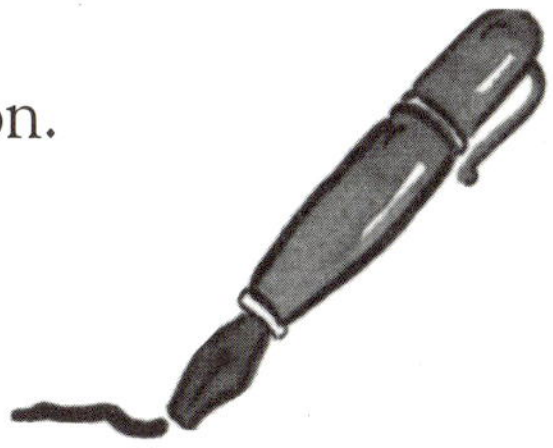

A biography of ....

Plan a play

On this page and on page 25 you can **plan** a **story**, which you will later turn into a **play**.

The **story** is titled *Finders Keepers*. It has five **characters** – three main **characters**, all children, and two minor adult **characters**.

The story is **set** in the present.
The events happen in three different places, all known to you.

The **story** begins after the three children find an old treasure map hidden in a mysterious old book bought at a school sale.

You decide what happens next, but remember that the **story** must be exciting and should keep the reader guessing before it reaches a happy ending.

To **plan** your **story**, complete the **storyboard** on this page and the next. Draw pictures in each box to show how the story **begins**, **develops** and **ends**. Number each picture, and write a short sentence to explain what is happening.

Storyboard

Title of play ....

Writer ....

....

....

Plan a play (continued)

Your stage

Use your **storyboard** on pages 24 and 25 to **plan** the **set** for your **play**.

Your stage looks like this. Draw in the **scenery**, or the **set**, for one **scene**.

Now make a list of the **props** (things actors wear, carry or use) needed for your **play**.

Props

....

....

....

....

....

Write your play

Look back over your notes on pages 24 to 26, then begin writing your **play** on this page. You will need to continue writing on other sheets of paper.

In the first column, write the **name** of each character as he or she speaks. Write their actual words in the middle column (you don't need speech marks). Use the right-hand column to write what you think should be happening on stage – these are your **production notes**.

Remember: Write – in brackets – after the character's name any **directions** about how that character speaks or moves.

Finders Keepers

A play in three scenes

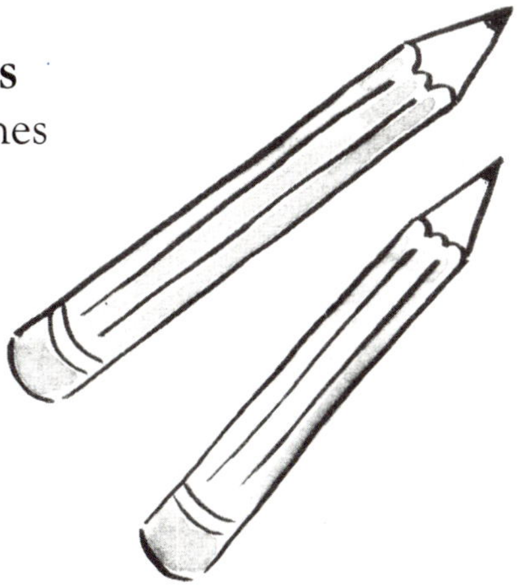

Characters in order of appearance

1 ....

2 ....

3 ....

4 ....

5 ....

Scene One

Characters	Script	Production notes

Looking at instructions

Look at these **instructions** from an activity book, then answer the questions. (You do not need to do the exercise yourself.)

You will need:
A sheet of paper
One blue felt-tip pen
One red felt-tip pen

Simple route map
1 Use the blue pen to draw the main roads between your house and a friend's house. Show where smaller roads join the main roads.

2 Draw a house or flat at either end of the route, and add any helpful landmarks, such as traffic lights, big trees, or a pond.

3 Write in each house's number and the names of the most important roads. Then use the red pen to draw a line of arrows to show the best route.

Why is it important to include the **you will need** section?

....

....

Underline all the words that tell you what to do. What kind of words are they?

....

Why might someone want to draw this map?

....

....

How do you know that these **instructions** were written for people of about your age?

....

....

Writing instructions

Write some **instructions** to help a friend make an "old treasure map". You will need to list the **materials** and **tools** needed for the job and also describe how to make the map look old.

Write clear, numbered **instructions** in the boxes.
Draw lines, called **leader lines**, from each instruction to the part of the map it refers to.

Make an Old Treasure Map

You will need: ....

....

Your map could look like this:

Instructions:

....
....
....
....

....
....
....
....

....
....
....
....

Concrete poetry

This **concrete poem** gives you a picture of a **saying**. What is the **saying**? What does it mean?

[I'M] [TALKING] [TO] [A] [BRICK] [TO] [A] [BRICK] [WALL]
[TALKING] [TO] [A] [BRICK] [WALL] [TO] [A] [BRICK] [WALL]
[I'M] [TALKING] [TO] [A] [BRICK] [WALL] [TO] [A] [BRICK]

This **concrete poem** represents another **saying**. Work out what it is, then explain its meaning.

wave!

I'm of I'm of a

on the crest a wave on the the crest

crest of on the wave of a crest of on crest on the

a I'm I'm crest a I'm of a I'm

wave on the wave wave

This **concrete poem** is also a **saying**. Can you see what it is? What does the **saying** mean?

g g

r r

N A g N A

S s KE g r E g S s KE g

s S r N A K S g S r KE s S r

N A S s N r E N A N A

s K E s A K s s KE...sss!

s s s s

Look back at the **concrete poems** on page 30, then use this space to write some **concrete poems** of your own. You can either use some of the **sayings** on page 8 or choose your own.

Word-wheels

How many words of four or more letters can you make from these **word-wheels**? Each word must have the letters that form the wheel's "hub" as its centre and one of the "rim" letters at the beginning and at the end.

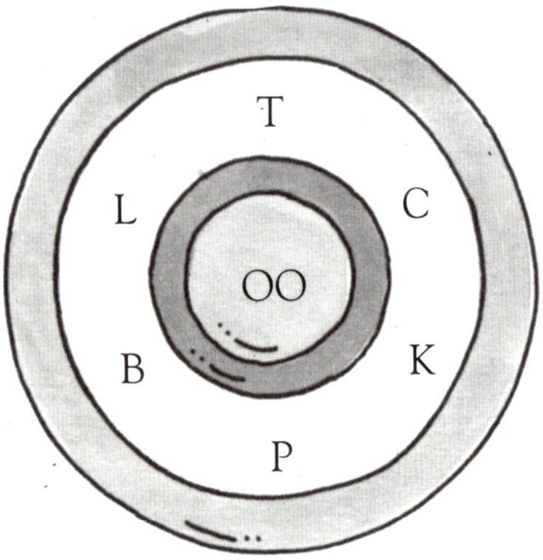

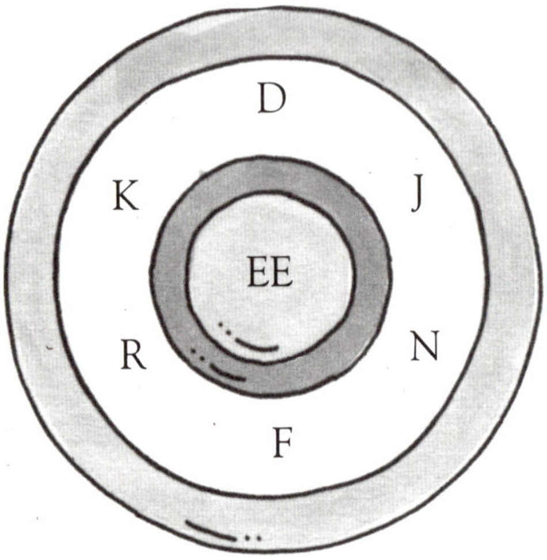

look, cool, book,

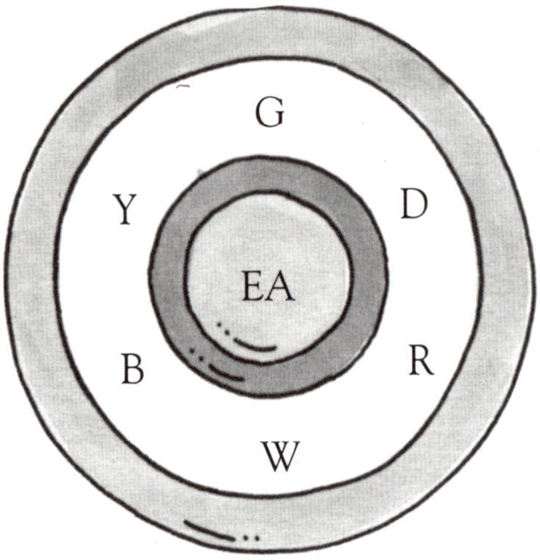

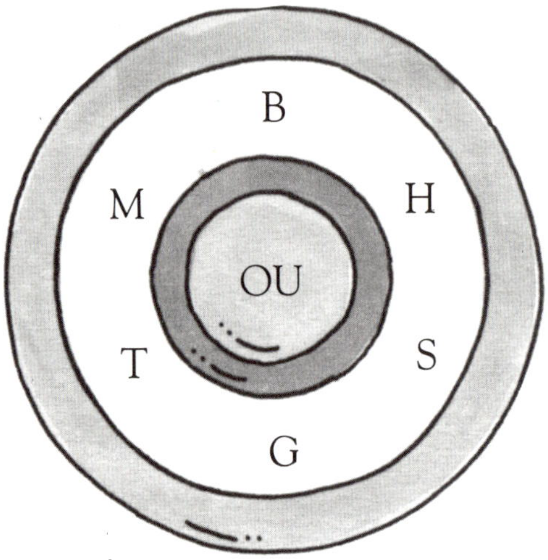

tough

Answer Section with Parents' Notes

Key Stage 2
Ages 9–10
Workbook 1

This 8-page section provides answers or explanatory notes to all the activities in this book. This will enable you to assess your child's work.

Point out any spelling mistakes, incorrect punctuation and grammatical errors as you mark each page. Also correct any handwriting errors. (Your child should use the handwriting style taught at his or her school.) As well as making corrections, it is very important to praise your child's efforts and achievements.

Encourage your child to use a dictionary, and suggest that he or she uses a notebook to compile a **word bank** of new words or difficult spellings.

2

Spelling patterns

Look at these words and the different ways their **plurals** are formed:

dog	dogs
kiss	kisses
dish	dishes
church	churches
knife	knives
fly	flies
boy	boys

Now write the **plurals** of the words below. Use the examples above as a guide. Check your answers in a dictionary. D
Remember: Plural means that there is more than one of something.

cat	cats	aunty	aunties
ash	ashes	berry	berries
batch	batches	cake	cakes
wife	wives	day	days
trolley	trolleys	monkey	monkeys
party	parties	hamster	hamsters
cry	cries	sash	sashes
toy	toys	arch	arches
tray	trays	leaf	leaves
key	keys	dolly	dollies
parrot	parrots	shanty	shanties
lash	lashes	try	tries
stitch	stitches	alloy	alloys
thief	thieves	bay	bays
lolly	lollies	chimney	chimneys

On this page your child revises the main spelling patterns used to form the plurals of nouns. If your child is unsure of an answer, encourage him or her to take a guess and then check in a dictionary.

3

More on plurals

Complete the following rules.

How to make plurals

1 For most **nouns**, simply add s
2 If the **noun** ends with **-s**, **-sh** or **-ch**, add es
3 For most **nouns** ending with an **-f**, change the **f** to v, and then add es.
4 If the **noun** ends with **-ly**, **-ry** or **-ty**, change the y to ie, and then add s.
5 If the **noun ends** with **-ay**, **-ey**, **-oy**, just add s

Find examples of **nouns** that end in each of the ways described above. Write the words as both **singular** and **plural** nouns.
Remember: A **noun** is a naming word.

1
2
3 Answers may vary
4
5

Peculiar plurals!
Add **-es** to these words.

potato	potatoes	echo	echoes	tomato	tomatoes

Add only **-s** to these words:

solo	solos	photo	photos	piano	pianos
Zulu	Zulus	banana	bananas	kiwi	kiwis

This page focuses on five rules that will help your child to form plurals. It may help your child to work out the answers if he or she refers back to the list on page 2. The final activity features some common words that do not follow these rules.

4

An alphabet of plurals

Can you write the **plurals** of the words in this alphabetical list? D

alley	alleys	net	nets
box	boxes	orange	oranges
calf	calves	pastry	pastries
donkey	donkeys	quarry	quarries
elf	elves	ray	rays
fairy	fairies	story	stories
gnu	gnus	torpedo	torpedoes
half	halves	umbrella	umbrellas
igloo	igloos	volcano	volcanoes
jelly	jellies	worry	worries
knight	knights	xylophone	xylophones
laugh	laughs	yacht	yachts
miss	misses	zoo	zoos

Rewrite these nonsense sentences, and make all the **nouns plural**. D
Remember: A **noun** is a naming word.

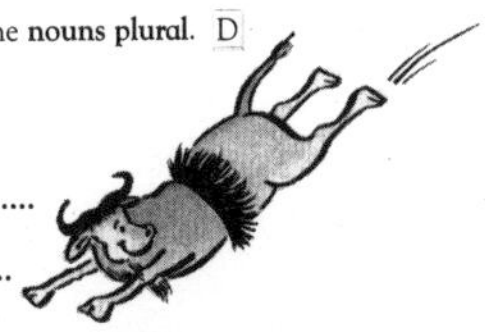

The gnu in a tutu flew past the Zulu.
The gnus in tutus flew past the Zulus.

The tomato sang a solo while playing the piano.
The tomatoes sang solos while playing pianos.

These fun activities help reinforce your child's knowledge of how to form plurals. Encourage your child to check his or her answers in a dictionary. In the last exercise, ensure that your child does not include the word *a* in his or her sentences.

5

Prefixes

Read the **definitions** below, and complete the explanation of each **prefix**. Check your answers in a dictionary. The first one has been done for you. D
Remember: A **prefix** is a group of letters added to the beginning of a word to change its meaning.

automatic: able to work by itself
autograph: a person's name written by him or herself

auto- means self

bicycle: a two-wheeled cycle
biped: a creature with two feet

bi- means two

telephone: an instrument for sending and receiving sounds over a distance
telescope: an instrument for making distant objects appear nearer

tele- means distant

transport: carry from one place to another
transform: change from one thing to another

trans- means change or cross

circumference: distance around a circle
circumnavigate: sail or fly around something

circum- means around

This activity will help your child learn about the meanings and uses of several common prefixes; it will also help your child with comprehension and spelling. If your child enjoys this exercise, ask him or her to find other words with the same prefixes.

6

A collection of synonyms

Use a **thesaurus** or a **dictionary** to help you find at least two words that are the same or similar in meaning to these words. D T
Remember: **Synonyms** are words that have the same or similar meanings.

happy cheerful, glad, delighted, pleased

sad unhappy, miserable

angry mad, cross, annoyed

calm smooth, peaceful, still

strong tough, powerful, fit

weak feeble, soft

rough hard, coarse, uneven, bumpy

smooth even, flat, level

quick speedy, rapid, swift, fast

slow leisurely, lethargic, sluggish

Answers may vary

For this activity on synonyms, a children's thesaurus, preferably one that is arranged alphabetically, will be particularly useful. Discuss the words your child chooses and the context in which it would be most appropriate to use each one.

7

Using synonyms

For each **adjective** listed below, write a sentence that uses at least two of the **synonyms** you wrote on page 6. Try to show the slight difference in meaning between your **synonyms**.

happy I was **pleased** with my card and **delighted** with my presents.

sad

angry

calm

strong

weak

rough

smooth

quick

slow

Answers may vary

The exercise on this page provides practice in using synonyms. By making up sentences, your child will discover the subtle differences between the meanings of synonyms. Discuss the reasoning behind your child's choices.

8

Sayings

Read these **sayings**, then explain what each one means.

out of the frying pan into the fire means ending up in a worse situation than the previous one

over the top means exaggerated or excessive

raining cats and dogs means that it is raining very hard

a storm in a teacup means a big fuss made over something that is unimportant

to blow your own trumpet means to praise yourself

to hit the nail on the head means to be absolutely correct about something

Answers may vary

Picture that!
Now imagine that these **sayings** mean exactly what the words say – that they are **literal** rather than **metaphorical.** Choose two of the **sayings**, and draw a picture to illustrate their **literal** meaning. Write each **saying** under its picture.

On this page, your child is asked to explain some common sayings, or idioms, and then to think about the actual words: the literal meaning rather than the metaphorical one. The drawings help to clarify the terms *literal* and *metaphorical.*

9

Word-building

The **root** of the words below is **perfect**.

perfection   im**perfect**   **perfect**ly

Underline the **roots** in these words.

admit   permit   transmit

dictionary   predict   dictate

fixture   prefix   suffix

Now add the **root** of the first word in each line to the other words in the line to build more words with the same **root**.

report	trans p o r t	ex p o r t	p o r t able
inform	in f o r m ation	trans f o r m	trans f o r m ation
defect	in f e c t	in f e c t ion	af f e c t ion

Use each word you built above in a **sentence** that shows you understand its meaning.

Answers may vary

The activities on this page focus on building words with a common root. Being aware of the roots in words is a valuable support for spelling and will help to extend your child's vocabulary.

10

Adverbs

Written dialogue can tell readers **how** things are said. Kenneth Grahame used these six **adverbs** in the following conversation from *The Wind in the Willows*: **slowly, triumphantly, wistfully, doggedly, loyally, imploringly.**

Decide where each word would make the best sense, and write it in place. D
Remember: Adverbs tell us more about the verbs in a sentence.

1 It was indeed very compact and comfortable. Little sleeping-bunks – a little table that folded up against the wall – a cooking-stove, lockers, bookshelves, a bird cage with a bird in it; and pots, pans, jugs and kettles of every size and variety.

2 "All complete!" said the Toad ......triumphantly...... , pulling open a locker. "You see – biscuits, potted lobster, sardines – everything you can possibly want. Soda-water here – baccy there – letter-paper, bacon, jam, cards and dominoes – you'll find," he continued, as they descended the steps again, "you'll find that nothing whatever has been forgotten, when we make our start this afternoon."

3 "I beg your pardon," said the Rat ......slowly...... , as he chewed a straw, "but did I overhear you say something about '*we*', and '*start*', and '*this afternoon*'?"

4 "Now, you dear good old Ratty," said Toad ......imploringly......, "don't begin talking in that stiff and sniffy sort of way, because you know you've *got* to come. I can't possibly manage without you, so please consider it settled, and don't argue – it's the one thing I can't stand. You surely don't mean to stick to your dull fusty old river all your life, and just live in a hole in a bank, and *boat*? I want to show you the world! I'm going to make an *animal* of you, my boy!"

5 "I don't care," said the Rat ......doggedly...... . "I'm not coming, and that's flat. And I *am* going to stick to my old river, *and* live in a hole, *and* boat, as I've always done. And what's more, Mole's going to stick to me and do as I do, aren't you, Mole?"

6 "Of course I am," said the Mole ......loyally...... . "I'll always stick to you, Rat, and what you say is to be – has got to be. All the same, it sounds as if it might have been – well, rather fun, you know!" he added ......wistfully...... . Poor Mole! The Life Adventurous was so new a thing to him and so thrilling; and this fresh aspect of it was so tempting; and he had fallen in love at first sight with the canary-coloured cart and all its little fitments.

This page features a piece of dialogue from *The Wind in the Willows*. Filling in the missing words will give your child practice in recognising and using adverbs. For each sentence, discuss the reason for your child's choice.

11

Tenses

Verbs tell us whether an event has already happened, is happening now or will happen later.

Past tense	**Present tense**	**Future tense**
Toad escaped ...	Toad escapes ...	Toad will escape ...
Toad was escaping ...	Toad is escaping ...	

Rewrite these sentences, and choose a **verb** in the **tense** suggested.

Toad (future) his car.

Rat (present) by the river.

Mole (past) the door.

He (past) the caravan canary-yellow.

Toad (future) from prison.

The stoats and weasels (future) all Toad's belongings.

Toad (past) the policeman.

Badger (present) in the Wild Wood.

Answers may vary

Your child needs to understand the differences between the past, present and future tenses. It may help if you discuss the sample sentences at the top of the page before your child begins. Accept any reasonable choice of verb in the correct tense.

12

Writing dialogue

Look back at page 10, then complete the following sentences.

When each character starts to s p e a k, a new p a r a g r a p h begins.

The actual words s p o k e n are enclosed in s p e e c h m a r k s, which are also called i n v e r t e d c o m m a s.

Verbs such as **said** and **remarked** are separated from the speaker's words by c o m m a s unless there are other punctuation marks in the speech.

When **reporting** what was said (rather than writing down the speaker's actual words) don't use s p e e c h m a r k s.

Now use **reported speech** to write out what Rat and Mole said in paragraphs 5 and 6 on page 10.
Remember: Reported speech is what you would use if you were telling someone else about the conversation.

The rat replied doggedly that he didn't care and he wasn't going. He was going to stick to his old river and live in a hole and a boat as he'd always done. He added that Mole was going to stick with him and do as he did.

Mole agreed. He said that he would always stick to Rat and that what Rat said was to be would be. But he added wistfully that it sounded as if it might have been fun.

This activity helps your child to recognise direct speech and to change it into reported speech. Check that your child has changed tenses where necessary and that, where any words are removed or added, the sense and sentence structure remain the same.

13 More reported speech

Use **reported speech** to rewrite paragraph 2 of *The Wind in the Willows* on page 10.

Toad said triumphantly that it was all complete, and he pulled open a locker. He said that there was everything they could possibly want – biscuits, potted lobster and sardines. As he descended the steps he added that there was soda-water, baccy, letter-paper, bacon, jam, cards and dominoes. He said that they would find that nothing whatsoever had been forgotten when they made their start that afternoon.

When you change the characters' actual words (**direct speech**) into **reported speech**, what happens to the **verbs**?

The verbs need to be changed to the past tense.

Did you have to change anything else?

I also had to change word order, add words such as 'that', and change some pronouns.

Correcting mistakes

Rewrite the sentences below, correcting the grammatical mistakes.

Toad said there wasn't nothing like it. It is the best pastime ever.

Toad said there was nothing like it. It was the best pastime ever.

At first Rat says he weren't going nowhere.

At first Rat said he wasn't going anywhere.

Rat and Mole was persuaded to take a trip in Toad's caravan.

Rat and Mole were persuaded to take a trip in Toad's caravan.

This page provides your child with more practice in writing reported speech and focuses his or her attention on the changes made to verbs and tenses. The second exercise helps your child recognise and correct common grammatical mistakes.

14 Starting a story

There are many different ways to **begin** a story. Kenneth Grahame starts *The Wind in the Willows* like this:

"The Mole had been working very hard all the morning, spring-cleaning his little home."

J. R. R. Tolkien's *The Hobbit* begins like this:

"In a hole in the ground there lived a hobbit. Not a nasty, dirty, wet hole, filled with the ends of worms and an oozy smell, nor yet a dry, bare, sandy hole with nothing in it to sit down on or to eat: it was a hobbit-hole, and that means comfort."

Robert Louis Stevenson begins *Treasure Island* like this:

"Squire Trelawney, Dr. Livesey, and the rest of these gentlemen having asked me to write down the whole particulars about Treasure Island, from the beginning to the end, ... "

Which of these novels begins in the **middle** of something happening?

The Wind in the Willows

Which story is told by a character **after** the story has happened?

Treasure Island

Which of these books starts with a **description** of the place where the story begins?

The Hobbit

This activity asks your child to investigate the opening paragraphs of three famous books. Help your child to realise that a story does not need to be told in strict chronological order and that original beginnings help capture a reader's interest.

15 Different beginnings

Supposing the writers of the stories discussed on page 14 had decided to **begin** their famous books differently, how might they have **begun**?

If you have read these books, write a different **beginning** for each one. Otherwise, choose stories that **begin** in similar ways, and use a different style to write a new **beginning** for each one.

The Wind in the Willows or ....

Answers may vary

The Hobbit or ....

Answers may vary

Treasure Island or ....

Answers may vary

The activity on this page builds on the work done on page 14. If your child is not familiar with the chosen books, discuss alternative stories that can be used instead; choosing favourite or familiar books may increase your child's enjoyment.

16 Characters

How do we get to know the **personality** of a **character** in a story? Tick the possible ways on this checklist.

- use the table of contents ☐
- character's description ✓
- what the character says ✓
- use the index ☐
- what other characters say ✓
- look at chapter headings ☐
- what the character does ✓
- how he or she treats others ✓
- look at the pictures ✓

Choose a **character** from a story you have read. Using the ways you have ticked in the checklist, make brief **notes** about the **character** here.

The character is called ....

He/she is in the story titled ....

written by ....

Notes

Answers may vary

This activity focuses on how fictional characters are constructed and presented. Point out that a character's actions can reveal his or her personality to the reader without the writer needing to slow down the action with lengthy descriptions.

17

Add an incident!

Reread the notes you made on page 16. Now **plan** and then write an extra **incident** in the life of the **character** you chose.

Hints:
First decide how this **incident** will show us more about the **character**.
Then decide on one or two other **characters** to take part in the **incident**.
Think of a good **moment** in the story for the incident to happen.
Think of a **title** for the **incident**.

.... (title)

Answers may vary

There is a lot to think about in this activity. Your child may need help in planning a new scene in order to develop the character. Check written work for consistency of style and character, for paragraphs and for details to interest the reader.

18

Patterns in a poem

Read this **poem** aloud.

The Land of Counterpane

When I was sick and lay a-bed,
I had two pillows at my head,
And all my toys beside me lay
To keep me happy all the day.

And sometimes for an hour or so
I watched my leaden soldiers go,
With different uniforms and drills,
Among the bed-clothes, through the hills;

And sometimes sent my ships in fleets
All up and down among the sheets;
Or brought my trees and houses out,
And planted cities all about.

I was the giant great and still
That sits upon the pillow-hill,
And sees before him dale and plain,
The pleasant land of counterpane.

Robert Louis Stevenson

This **poem** has a regular **rhythm**. Count the number of **beats** (syllables) in each line.

The number of **beats** in each line of the poem is 8

The Land of Counterpane has a simple pattern of **rhymes**.

Describe the **rhyming** scheme (pattern) of this poem.
This poem is written in rhyming couplets.

Make a list of this poem's **rhyming pairs**.
a-bed-head, lay-day, so-go, drills-hills, fleets-sheets, out-about, still-hill, plain-counterpane

This page, together with the following two pages, examines the poetic style of Robert Louis Stevenson. Encourage your child to read the poems aloud, with expression, before looking more closely to note down the rhythm and rhyme.

19

More patterns in a poem

Read this **poem** aloud.

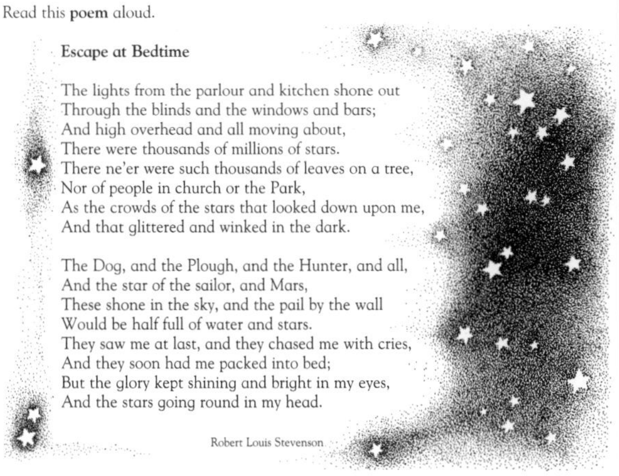

Escape at Bedtime

The lights from the parlour and kitchen shone out
Through the blinds and the windows and bars;
And high overhead and all moving about,
There were thousands of millions of stars.
There ne'er were such thousands of leaves on a tree,
Nor of people in church or the Park,
As the crowds of the stars that looked down upon me,
And that glittered and winked in the dark.

The Dog, and the Plough, and the Hunter, and all,
And the star of the sailor, and Mars,
These shone in the sky, and the pail by the wall
Would be half full of water and stars.
They saw me at last, and they chased me with cries,
And they soon had me packed into bed;
But the glory kept shining and bright in my eyes,
And the stars going round in my head.

Robert Louis Stevenson

There are two **rhythmic patterns** in *Escape at Bedtime*. The two numbers of **beats** (syllables) in the poem are 11 and 9.

Escape at Bedtime has a slightly different **rhyming scheme** from *The Land of Counterpane* on page 18. Describe the **rhyming scheme** of *Escape at Bedtime*.
The rhyming scheme of Escape at Bedtime is AB AB CD CD etc

Make a list of this poem's **rhyming pairs**.
out-about, bars-stars, tree-me, Park-dark, all-wall, Mars-stars, cries-eyes, bed-head

Can you find anything in the two **poems** to suggest they were written by the same poet?
Both poems are set in a child's bedroom, and they are both about a child's thoughts and imaginings. The poems both have regular rhythms.

This poem has a more complex rhythmic pattern. If your child does not know the alphabetical method of expressing a rhyming scheme, accept any answer that shows understanding. Both poems are about a lone child using his imagination.

20

Looking at poems

Reread the **poem** *The Land of Counterpane* on page 18, then answer these questions.

Counterpane is an old-fashioned word. What is a counterpane? D
A counterpane is a quilt or a bedspread.

Name the metal from which the toy soldiers were made. Explain why you think this metal is no longer used for making toys.
The toy soldiers were made of lead. Toys are not made of this metal today because it is poisonous and because plastic is cheaper.

Why does the boy call himself "the giant"?
The boy feels gigantic, towering over his tiny toy soldiers.

What do the words **dale** and **plain** mean? D
A dale is a valley
A plain is a wide, flat stretch of land.

Now reread the **poem** *Escape at Bedtime* on page 19, and answer these questions.

What is a parlour? D
A parlour is a sitting room.

The number of stars is compared with three things in the speaker's own experience. What are they?
The number of stars is compared to leaves on a tree and people in a church or a park.

Explain what is meant by "The Dog, and the Plough, and the Hunter".
The Dog, the Plough, and the Hunter are constellations of stars.

Which words tell you that when he went to bed, he remembered the way the sky looked?
But the glory kept shining and bright in my eyes,
And the stars going round in my head.

This comprehension activity will test your child's understanding of the two poems. Encourage your child to use a dictionary to check the meaning of the old-fashioned words; he or she is not expected to already know the meanings of the words.

21 Reading and understanding

Read this **biography** of Robert Louis Stevenson, then answer the following questions in full sentences.

Robert Louis Stevenson was born in Edinburgh, Scotland, in the middle of the nineteenth century. His father was an engineer, well known for designing and building lighthouses. Robert was to become even more famous than his father, not as an engineer, but as an author.

When he was young, Robert's family hoped that he would follow in his father's footsteps, but very poor health made this impossible. Even as a child, Robert was often ill and had to spend a great deal of time in bed.

As a young man, Robert Louis Stevenson studied law and qualified as a barrister, but having set his heart on becoming an author, he put all his efforts into writing.

As an adult, he continued to suffer from tuberculosis, a serious chest ailment, and spent much time travelling in Europe and America, seeking warmer climates, where he thought his health might improve.

In 1880, after marrying in California, he and his wife returned to England. They settled there for a while, until in 1888, they went off to the South Pacific. Finally, the Stevensons settled in Samoa, and at first, Robert felt much healthier.

In 1894, however, the man whose books were loved by many throughout the world and who was called Tusitala (the storyteller) by the Samoan Islanders, died suddenly.

Robert Louis Stevenson wrote stories, poems, travel books and several novels. Two of his most famous books are *Treasure Island* and *Kidnapped*. Many of the poems from *A Child's Garden of Verses* are well known and well loved, remaining popular today, over one hundred years after Robert Louis Stevenson first wrote them.

Why is Robert Louis Stevenson famous?

Robert Louis Stevenson is a famous writer. He wrote novels such as Treasure Island, as well as many poems.

When and where was he born, and when and where did he die?

He was born in Edinburgh, Scotland, in the middle of the nineteenth century.

He died in Samoa in 1894.

Why did Robert Louis Stevenson often have to stay in bed when he was a boy?

He often had to stay in bed as a boy because he suffered from tuberculosis.

This brief biography of Robert Louis Stevenson shows the way in which his experiences affected his work. Help your child to make the link between the poet's poor health and his poems written about a boy in bed.

22 Reading and understanding

Read the **biography** of Robert Louis Stevenson on page 21 again, then answer the following questions.

Why did Robert Louis Stevenson travel to different countries?

Stevenson travelled to find warmer climates to improve his health.

Where did he go in 1888?

In 1888 he went to the South Pacific.

Why do you think he was called **Tusitala**?

He was called Tusitala because he told good stories.

Explain what these **expressions** mean:

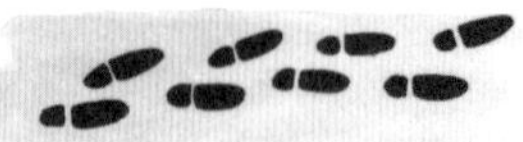

follow in his father's footsteps

take up the same career as his father

set his heart on

was determined to become

What do you notice about the way the events in Robert Louis Stevenson's life are arranged on the page?

There is a new paragraph for each idea or each stage in his life.

This is a short **biography** of Robert Louis Stevenson. Give the meaning of the word **biography**. If necessary, use a dictionary. D

A biography is the story of someone's life.

Now make up **three extra questions** that could be answered by using this **biography**.

Answers may vary

These questions require a lot of attention to the details in the biography on page 21. Encourage your child to use a dictionary to check the meaning of the word *biography*.

23 Write a biography

Using the **biography** on page 21 as a guide, write your own **biography** about a famous person who interests you. You will need to make short **notes** from **reference** books, **CD-ROMs,** the **Internet** or your own knowledge. Take **notes** from more than one place if possible.
Remember: Use a new **paragraph** for each new point of information.

A biography of ....

Answers may vary

This activity will take a while to complete as it requires research, note-taking and planning. Check that your child's work has an introduction, follows a logical order and is broken into distinct paragraphs.

24 Plan a play

On this page and on page 25 you can **plan** a **story**, which you will later turn into a **play**.

The **story** is titled *Finders Keepers*. It has five **characters** – three main **characters**, all children, and two minor adult **characters**.

The story is **set** in the present.
The events happen in three different places, all known to you.

The **story** begins after the three children find an old treasure map hidden in a mysterious old book bought at a school sale.

You decide what happens next, but remember that the **story** must be exciting and should keep the reader guessing before it reaches a happy ending.

To **plan** your **story**, complete the **storyboard** on this page and the next. Draw pictures in each box to show how the story **begins**, **develops** and **ends**. Number each picture, and write a short sentence to explain what is happening.

Storyboard

Title of play Finders Keepers

Writer ....

Answers may vary

The activity on this and the following page introduces the idea of using a storyboard to plan written work, in this case a story that will be turned into a play. Explain to your child that planning has a purpose: it makes writing easier.

25 Plan a play (continued)

....

Answers may vary

This pages carries on from page 24. Encourage your child to plan what will happen in each box before spending time drawing and colouring pictures. This will prevent him or her needing to change the illustrations later on.

26 Your stage

Use your **storyboard** on pages 24 and 25 to **plan** the **set** for your **play**.

Your stage looks like this. Draw in the **scenery**, or the **set**, for one **scene**.

Now make a list of the **props** (things actors wear, carry or use) needed for your **play**.

Props

Answers may vary

Ask your child to choose one scene from his or her completed storyboard (pages 24–25) and to plan the set for that scene. Encourage your child to think carefully about what props the actors will need. Discuss the difference between props and scenery.

27 Write your play

Look back over your notes on pages 24 to 26, then begin writing your **play** on this page. You will need to continue writing on other sheets of paper.

In the first column, write the **name** of each character as he or she speaks. Write their actual words in the middle column (you don't need speech marks). Use the right-hand column to write what you think should be happening on stage – these are your **production notes**.

Remember: Write – in brackets – after the character's name any **directions** about how that character speaks or moves.

Finders Keepers

A play in three scenes

Characters in order of appearance

1 ....

2 ....

3 ....

4 ....

5 ....

Scene One

Characters	Script	Production notes

Answers may vary

Your child will need several sheets of paper. Ensure that your child uses his or her storyboard as a plan and that he or she sets out the playscript as it is on this page. The production notes indicate the actors' actions, e.g., *Ellen leans over and grabs the key.*

28 Looking at instructions

Look at these **instructions** from an activity book, then answer the questions. (You do not need to do the exercise yourself.)

You will need:
A sheet of paper
One blue felt-tip pen
One red felt-tip pen

Simple route map

1 Use the blue pen to draw the main roads between your house and a friend's house. Show where smaller roads join the main roads.

2 Draw a house or flat at either end of the route, and add any helpful landmarks, such as traffic lights, big trees, or a pond.

3 Write in each house's number and the names of the most important roads. Then use the red pen to draw a line of arrows to show the best route.

Why is it important to include the **you will need** section?

The "you will need" section makes sure that the reader has everything they will need before they begin.

Underline all the words that tell you what to do. What kind of words are they?

The words that tell you what to do are verbs.

Why might someone want to draw this map?

The map could be used to show a friend or a friend's parent how to get to your house.

How do you know that these **instructions** were written for people of about your age?

I can tell the instructions were for someone my age because the language is at my level and the illustrations are fun. Answers may vary

In this activity, your child is asked to read and evaluate instructions. Discuss the key elements in writing clear instructions: start with a list of the equipment needed, number each point, be concise and give information in the correct sequence.

29

Writing instructions

Write some **instructions** to help a friend make an "old treasure map". You will need to list the **materials** and **tools** needed for the job and also describe how to make the map look old.

Write clear, numbered **instructions** in the boxes.
Draw lines, called **leader lines**, from each instruction to the part of the map it refers to.

Make an Old Treasure Map

You will need: ....

Your map could look like this:

Instructions:

Answers may vary

On this page your child practises writing instructions and drawing leader lines (lines linking a caption with part of a diagram). Tell your child how to make paper look old by ripping it, crumpling it and dipping it in cold, black tea.

30

Concrete poetry

This **concrete poem** gives you a picture of a **saying**. What is the **saying**? What does it mean?

[I'M] [TALKING] [TO] [A] [BRICK] [TO] [A] [BRICK] [WALL]
[TALKING] [TO] [A] [BRICK] [WALL] [TO] [A] [BRICK] [WALL]
[I'M] [TALKING] [TO] [A] [BRICK] [WALL] [TO] [A] [BRICK]

The saying is "talking to a brick wall", which means talking to someone who gives no response.

This **concrete poem** represents another **saying**. Work out what it is, then explain its meaning.

wave!
I'm of I'm of a
on the crest a wave on the the crest
crest of on the wave of a crest of on crest on the
a I'm I'm crest a I'm of a I'm
wave on the wave wave

The saying "I'm on the crest of a wave" means that I am being carried along by something good that is happening in my life.

This **concrete poem** is also a **saying**. Can you see what it is? What does the **saying** mean?

g g
r r
N A g N A
S s KE g r E g S s KE g
s S r N A K S g S r KE s S r
N A S s N r E N A N A
s K E s A K s s KE...sss!
s s s s

The saying is "a snake in the grass", which refers to a danger that is hidden.

This fun activity looks at how words can be combined with art to help create an image in a reader's mind. Point out to your child that each poem is an example of a metaphor; this will help him or her complete the exercise on page 31.

31

Look back at the **concrete poems** on page 30, then use this space to write some **concrete poems** of your own. You can either use some of the **sayings** on page 8 or choose your own.

Answers may vary

Your child can use this page to have fun writing some "concrete" poems. A good starting point would be to think of common metaphors, similes or sayings, such as *hit the nail on the head* or *as tall as a tree.*

32

Word-wheels

How many words of four or more letters can you make from these **word-wheels**? Each word must have the letters that form the wheel's "hub" as its centre and one of the "rim" letters at the beginning and at the end.

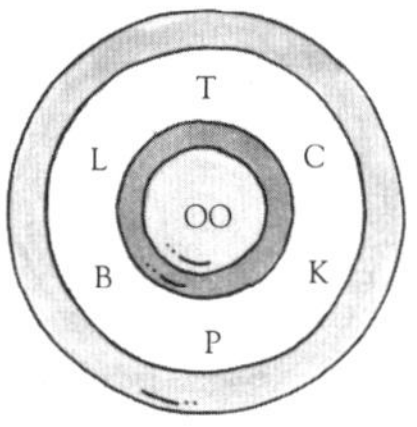

look, cool, book,
boot, pool, tool, loot

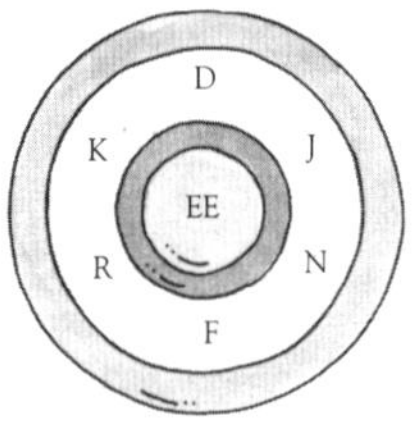

feed, deer, jeer, reef, need, freed

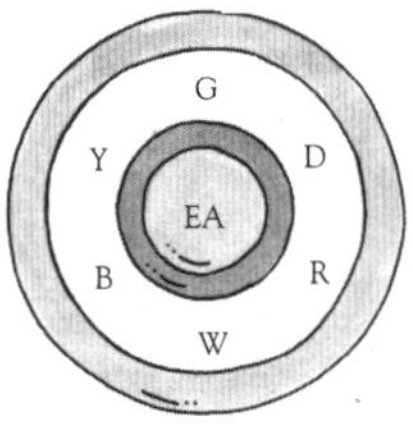

gear, dear, year, bear, wear,
read, bead, beard, bread

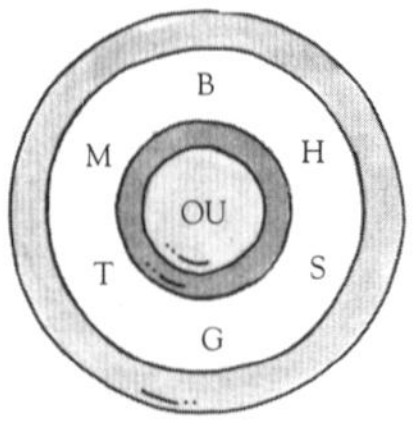

tough
bough, mouth, shout, bought

On this page your child practises using his or her visual skills to recognise patterns in the way letters combine to form words. Accept any words that follow the rules and that can be found in a dictionary.